WHAT

There Is a FIRE?

by Anara Guard

illustrated by Gina Pfleegor

PICTURE WINDOW BOOKS
a capstone imprint

Thanks to our adviser for his expertise and advice:
Terry Flaherty, PhD
Professor of English
Minnesota State University, Mankato

Editor: Shelly Lyons
Designer: Ashlee Suker
Art Director: Nathan Gassman
Production Specialist: Sarah Bennett
The illustrations in this book were created with oil paint and colored pencils.

Picture Window Books
151 Good Counsel Drive
P.O. Box 669
Mankato, MN 56002-0669
877-845-8392
www.capstonepub.com

All books published by Picture Window Books
are manufactured with paper containing at least
10 percent post-consumer waste.

Library of Congress Cataloging-in-Publication Data
 Guard, Anara.
What if there is a fire? / by Anara Guard ; illustrated by Gina Pfleegor.
p. cm. — (Danger zone)
Includes index.
ISBN 978-1-4048-6685-0 (library binding)
ISBN 978-1-4048-7033-8 (paperback)
1. Fire prevention—Juvenile literature. 2. Safety
education—Juvenile literature. I. Pfleegor, Gina. II. Title.
III. Series.
TH9148.G83 2012
628.9'22—dc22   2011006551

Printed in the United States of America in North Mankato, Minnesota.
032011   006110CGF11

What if there was a fire? Would you know what to do? Fires are dangerous and can be scary, but you can be prepared. The stories in this book will help you know what to do in a fire. Follow the safety tips to be smart about fire.

How Do You Prepare for a Fire?

There are lots of ways to prepare for a fire. Daniel and his family check the smoke detectors every month.

Daniel's dad also checks the fire extinguisher.

Together the family draws an escape plan. The plan shows the best ways to get out of the house.

Our Escape Plan

SAFETY TIP

Get ready! Make an escape plan:
- With a parent, draw a map of your home. Mark all doors and windows.
- Draw arrows marking two ways out of each room. The main exit should always be a door.
- Choose an outdoor meeting place.
- Practice the plan with your family.

5

What If the Smoke Detector Goes Off at Home?

One night a loud noise wakes up Jessica. It's the smoke detector! Rascal starts barking. The air is thick with smoke, and Jessica coughs. She wants to hide, but she remembers to crawl to the door.

SAFETY TIP

Get low and go! If you smell or see smoke, you should drop to the floor. Smoke rises, so the air near the floor will be best for breathing.

Jessica touches the door. It feels cool, so she knows it's safe to open.

SAFETY TIP

Feel for fire! In a fire, always touch the door before opening it. If the door is cool, it's likely safe to open. A hot door means there could be fire on the other side. To get out, use a different exit or window.

In the hallway, Jessica's mother takes her hand. They hurry outside.

Where is her dad? Where is Rascal?

9

Jessica and her mother run to their
meeting place across the street.

Her father is there. He calls 911.

Jessica wants to go find Rascal. But her mom says they must stay outside.

Soon sirens wail and lights flash. Before long a firefighter brings Rascal to them. He tells them the fire is out.

SAFETY TIP

Get out and stay out! When you get to your outdoor meeting place, call 911. Do not go back into the building for any reason.

11

What If the Fire Alarm Goes Off at School?

Sam's class is listening to Mr. Martinez when the fire alarm sounds. Mr. Martinez tells everyone to form a line. He tells them to leave the building but not to run.

SAFETY TIP

Chill out! It's important to stay calm in a fire. When you keep your cool, you remember what to do.

Every class has a special place to meet.
Sam's class meets near the swings.

Sam is scared. But the firefighters tell them
it was a false alarm. It is safe to go back inside.

What If a Fire Starts on the Stove?

The pot catches on fire when Jamie's mother is cooking. Using the fire extinguisher, she sprays the flames. Soon the fire is gone.

Later, Jamie asks, "What if we didn't have an extinguisher?"

"We would go outside and call 911," Jamie's mom says.
"Firefighters would put out the fire." She hugs Jamie.

Jamie is glad they are safe.

What If a Friend Has Matches?

Mike and Carlos like to play in their fort. One day Mike wants a campfire. He lights a match. "Ouch!" he cries as he drops the match.

Carlos and Mike run to get help. They tell Carlos' dad about the fire.

Carlos' dad puts out the fire. But the fort is already ruined.

19

That night, Carlos' dad says, "Matches and lighters are not for kids. If you see them, come tell me right away."

"I should have told Mike to give you the matches," says Carlos.

"Next time you'll know what to do," Carlos' dad says. "I'm just glad you're both OK!"

Fires can be scary. But you can stay safe by following these rules:

- Get ready! Test smoke detectors and fire extinguishers. Make an escape plan.

- Get low and go! If there's smoke, crawl on the floor to get out.

- Feel for fire! Touch the door. If it's hot, don't open it.

- Get out and stay out! Go to your family's meeting place outdoors. Stay there until firefighters say it's safe to go back into the building.

- Chill out! Staying calm in a fire helps you remember what to do.

- Keep a fire extinguisher handy! But ask an adult to handle it.

- Don't play with fire! If you see something that could start a fire, tell an adult.

Danger! Danger!

This kitchen is full of fire dangers. Can you find four things that could start a fire? How about something that might put out a fire?

Ask a parent to join you on a trip around your own home. Are there any fire dangers?

Could start a fire: 1. the pot boiling over on the stove; 2. the candle; 3. the matches; 4. the overloaded electrical outlet
Could put out a fire: the fire extinguisher

GLOSSARY

escape plan—a map of a home that shows all the doors and windows to be used as exits in a fire

false alarm—when a fire alarm sounds but there is no fire

fire extinguisher—a holder with water and chemicals inside it; people use fire extinguishers to put out fires

smoke detector—a machine that senses smoke and warns people by making a loud sound

MORE BOOKS TO READ

Donahue, Jill Urban. *Contain the Flame: Outdoor Fire Safety*. How to Be Safe! Minneapolis: Picture Window Books, 2009.

Johnson, Jinny. *Being Safe*. Now We Know About. New York: Crabtree Pub. Company, 2010.

Rau, Dana Meachen. *Fire Safety*. Safe Kids. New York: Marshall Cavendish Benchmark, 2009.

INTERNET SITES

FactHound offers a safe, fun way to find Internet sites related to this book. All of the sites on FactHound have been researched by our staff.

Here's all you do:

Visit *www.facthound.com*

Type in this code: 9781404866850

Check out projects, games and lots more at
www.capstonekids.com

ABOUT THE AUTHOR

Anara Guard is a short story writer and poet who has worked in the field of injury prevention since 1993. She speaks around the country on a variety of topics related to unintentional and intentional injury. For seven years, she worked for the Children's Safety Network, a national injury and violence prevention resource center. Ms. Guard has also been a parent educator and a librarian. She has a master's degree in library and information science and a certificate in maternal and child health. The mother of two grown sons, she lives and writes in California.

INDEX